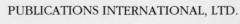

Look and Find

DINOSAURS

Cretaceous Corners • B.C. Junior High
Bucky Bee's Pizza Hive
Survival of the Fittest Health Spa
and more!

Illustrations
and Script Development
by Bob Terrio

Illustration Assistant: Gale Terrio

Louis Weber, C.E.O.
Publications International, Ltd.
7373 N. Cicero Avenue
Lincolnwood, Illinois 60646

PUBLICATIONS INTERNATIONAL, LTD.

Welcome to Cretaceous Corners! My name's Manny Tyranny and this is where I live. Have a look around and find out what my town is like. While you're at it, try to find me, my friends, and these other folks who live here with us.

Manny Tyranny

Sherri Topsian

Perry Saurolophus

Betty Bibliosaurus

Doc Rock

Officer Al O'Saurus

Floyd Trimmer

Mayor Patty Cephalosaur

These young dinosaurs go to school just like kids today do. But at B.C. Junior High, they study some pretty strange subjects. Spend some time in these dinosaur classrooms to see what they're like, and see if you can find these academic people and things.

Principal Franklin Fossil

Zippy the school mascot

Professor Pauli Ontology

Dean Dino

Terry Anasaur

John Dwanaland

The school bell

Reginald Preppie

For dinosaurs, it really is a jungle out there. To make it through the day, we've got to keep fit. Many dinosaurs come to me, Trainersaurus Rex, to get that extra edge they need. See if you can find me, and then try to find these other dinosaurs who like to pump iron and feel the burn at the Survival of the Fittest Health Spa.

Trainersaurus Rex

Icky Theosaur

Arnold Schwarzendino

Glenda Gladiator

Richard Simmonodon

Jayne Fondasaur

Mike Musclehead

Nadine Nautilusaur

What a beautiful Saturday afternoon! And there's no better place to spend it than here at Triassic Park. This place has everything a young dinosaur could want and more. The best part is that all my friends are here, too. See if you can find me, Perry Saurolophus, and then find all my fun-loving friends.

Perry Saurolophus

Angela Saurus

Sam Dunkasaur

Manny Tyranny

Sherri Topsian

Archie Opteryx

Buster Brachiosaur

Troy O'Don

Look at 'em go! These dinosaurs really know how to travel, don't they? Trains, planes, cars, trucks, boats, rockets—they've got every wild contraption you can imagine and then some! While they're zooming by, see if you can find these prehistoric speedsters.

Mad Maxine

Capt. Moe Zasore

Mario Andrettisaur

Charlie Limburger

The Red-winged Baron

Pirate Jean LaFoot

Chuck Yeagasaur

Daredevil Supersaurus Dave

BE MY HONEY

RAP TILES

Bucky Bee's—where a dinosaur can be a dinosaur! Dinosaur kids of all ages love to come here for the food, for the games, for the music, and for the fun. See if you can find these characters who are here for a party and find the birthday things they've brought with them.

Joy Stickasaur

Rocky road ice cream

ROCKY ROAD

Wanda Waitresaurus

Chef Crusty

This birthday present

This birthday cake

Nanny Tyrannus

Bucky Bee

KICK ME

WHACK A CAVEMAN

This is the biggest musical event in history, and you've got a front row seat for the entire show! All the top dinosaur performers have come for a day of nothing but fun and music, and they're ready to rock. Before the show starts, see if you can find these dinosaur superstars.

MC Lophysis

Madonnasaur

Cross Chris

Billy Ray Ceratops

Whitney Hadrosaur

Tyrannis Presley

Bruce Stegasteen

Cheradactyl

The Swamp Street Market is one of Sherri Topsian's favorite places. Anything and everything a dinosaur could possibly need is here to be bought, sold, or traded. There's just so much to do, so much to see, and so much to BUY!!! See if you can find Sherri and her friends, and then find these other buyers and sellers.

Sherri Topsian

Perry Saurolophus

Manny Tyranny

Velma Seraptor

Edmond Tonia

Lou Fangosaur

Charles Chargeit

Guy O. Cephaley

ROCK GARDEN

MARSHALL'S FOSSILS

WOOLY'S WORTHLESS DOO-DADS

J MART

CAR WASH

STICK SHIFT

HONK

QUACK

IT'S A FAMILY HAIR-LOOM

SWAMP BUGGIES

I KNEW SOME DAY MY PRINTS WOULD COME!

ROCKS 5TH AVENUE

IT'S YOU!

PET ROCKS

TYRANNO-SAURUS ROCKS

CASH ONLY!

JUICE

HUNTING STUFF

PIZZA

RED HOT BAR-B-Q'S

The mayor of Cretaceous Corners is a pachycephalosaur, or "thick-headed lizard." These dinosaurs had extremely thick, hard skulls, and scientists think they may have butted heads together the way sheep and deer do today. Go back to the town square and see if you can find these other hard things.

- [ ] A diamond
- [ ] A hard hat
- [ ] A hard rock musician
- [ ] A hard-working chef
- [ ] A "hard" roll
- [ ] Two hard-hitting boxers
- [ ] A "hard" wood tree
- [ ] A hard snowman

A map of Earth when dinosaurs first appeared would show that all the land was joined in a single continent called Pangaea. Pangaea slowly broke apart into two land masses, Laurasia and Gondwanaland, and they slowly separated into the continents we see on our maps today. Find these things that have to do with maps and directions back at the school.

- [ ] A treasure map
- [ ] A compass
- [ ] A globe
- [ ] A weather vane
- [ ] A police officer directing traffic
- [ ] A street sign
- [ ] An exit sign
- [ ] A "This side up" sign

Throughout this book, you've seen dinosaurs doing things that real dinosaurs never did. You've also seen some creatures that real dinosaurs never saw because the creatures probably didn't appear on Earth until after the dinosaurs were extinct. See if you can find these creatures back at the Swamp Street Market.

- [ ] A saber-toothed tiger
- [ ] A mammoth
- [ ] A rhinoceros
- [ ] A hippopotamus
- [ ] A caveman
- [ ] A dog
- [ ] A horse
- [ ] A mouse

All dinosaurs lived on land and moved about by walking and running. Dinosaurs like *Tyrannosaurus* always moved on two feet. Dinosaurs like *Triceratops* always moved on four feet. Dinosaurs like *Corythosaurus* probably moved on four feet most of the time but ran on two feet. See if you can find these foot things in the scene with all the vehicles.

- [ ] A football
- [ ] A "foot" hill
- [ ] Cowboy boots
- [ ] Socks
- [ ] A hotfoot
- [ ] Footprints
- [ ] "Foot" lights
- [ ] A "footnote"